JANE JOHNSON

My Dear Noel

The Story of a Letter from Beatrix Potter

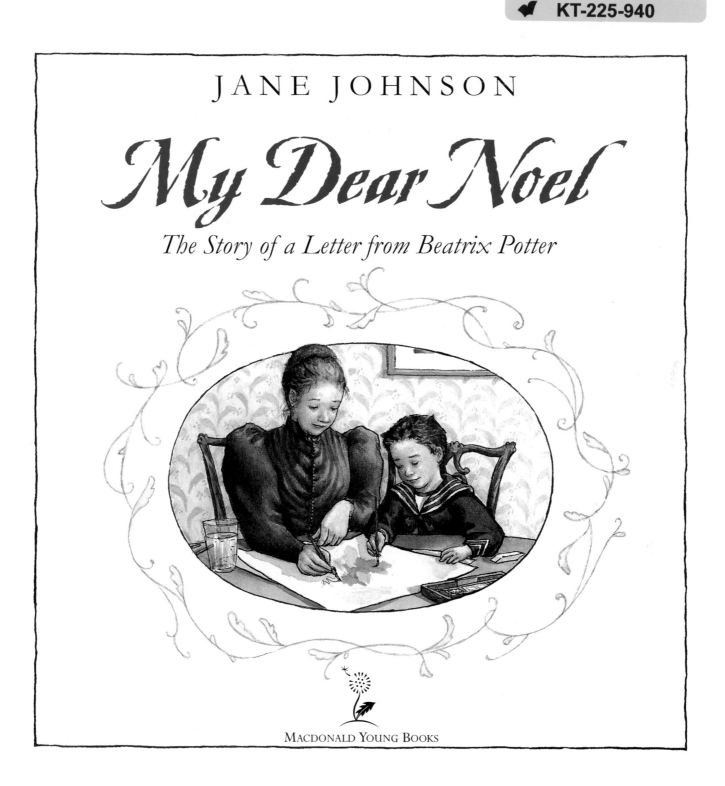

MACDONALD YOUNG BOOKS

For my mother

First published in 1999 in the US by
Dial Books for Young Readers
A member of Penguin Putnam Inc.
375 Hudson Street
New York, New York 10014

First published in 1999 in Great Britain by
Macdonald Young Books
an imprint of Wayland Publishers Ltd
61 Western Road
Hove
East Sussex
BN3 1JD

The author gratefully acknowledges Judy Taylor's book *Letters to Children*,
published by Frederick Warne, 1992, for its invaluable information
regarding the Moore family.

Printed in Hong Kong

ISBN: 0 7500 2847 5

hoe amongst the potatoes.
he ran on four legs &
that I think he would

altogether, if he had not
into a gooseberry net
fast by the large buttons
was a blue jacket with
new.

et &
the

Flopsy, Mopsy & Cottontail, who were good
little rabbits went down the lane to gather
blackberries, but Peter, who was very naughty

Peter was ill during the evening, in consequence
of over eating himself. His mother put him to
bed and gave him a dose of camomile tea,

"Miss Potter's coming today!" shouted Noel as he tumbled out of bed to tell the others.

All the Moore children loved Miss Potter's visits. But Noel had known her the longest, so he felt she belonged to him more than to Eric or Marjorie or Freda.

She spent so many hours alone in her room at the top of a big silent house that Noel was sure Miss Potter had much more fun with his family.

"Mama, is Miss Potter having *her* breakfast now?" Noel asked.

Before she could answer, the others began: "Will she bring her mice?" "I want to stroke her rabbit!"

"Wait and see, and don't all talk at once, dears."

When Noel had finished lessons with Mama, Nanny fetched the children's hats and they all streamed through the garden gate on to the common.

I must find something to give Miss Potter, Noel thought.

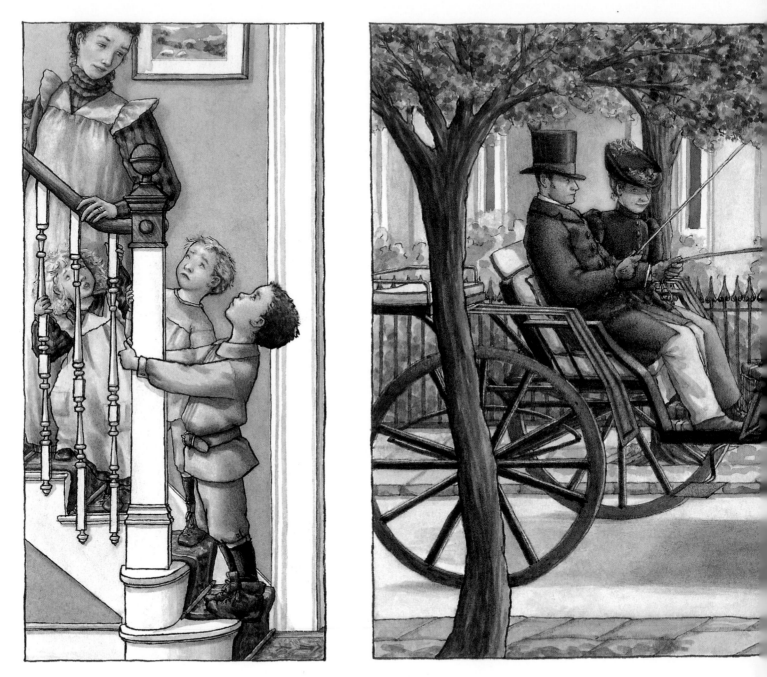

After lunch Mama said, "Now we'll have a rest before Miss Potter comes," and even though they fussed, she bundled everyone up to bed.

As Noel's eyes closed, he murmured, "Miss Potter's on her way."

"Oh, it's *lovely* to see all of you!" cried Miss Potter, running up the path. "Is this for me, Noel? What a wonderful colour. I shall wear it in my hat."

Then, opening Miss Potter's packages, they discovered treats for everyone – even the new baby who had not yet arrived.

Miss Potter's rabbit, Peter, and her mice forgot the tricks she'd taught them and were naughty instead.

Miss Potter laughed, the children shrieked and no one scolded

She told jokes that made
them ache with giggles.
 She drew pictures and never
said, "I'm tired, that's enough!"

Later, when Noel had Miss
Potter to himself, she whispered,
"I am going to Scotland soon,
so I shan't see you for a while.
But I *shall* write."

When the time came, Noel could hardly bear to see Miss Potter go.
After a last goodbye, Mama said, "Now, I expect you all to tidy up."
"I'm hot, and my head hurts," grumbled Noel.

"It might just be the excitement and too much cake," said his mother anxiously.

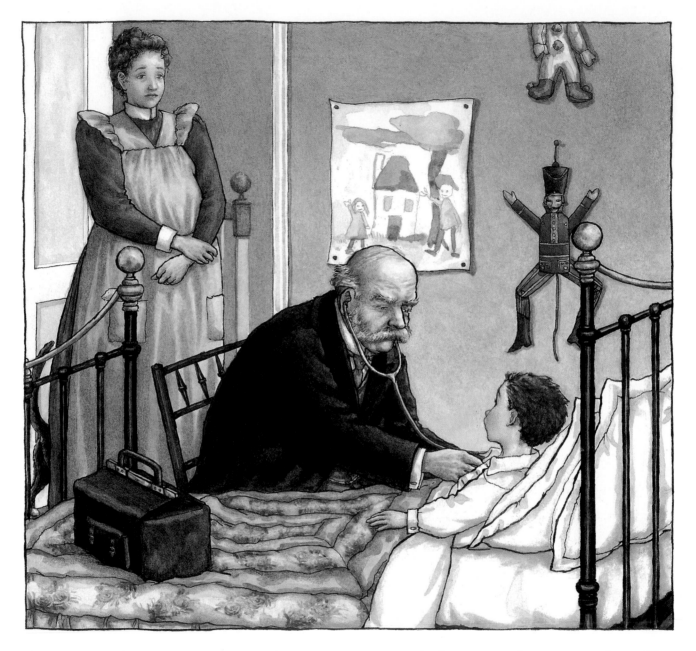

But in the morning Noel was worse and, because he was often ill, he knew he would have to stay in bed a long, long time.

Slowly the days dragged by. Gazing out of the window, Noel listened to the sounds of breakfast, lessons and then the shouts on the common as the others played.

"Miss Potter would know how to cheer him, Mrs. Moore –
I'm kept so busy with the younger ones," said Nanny.
"And I'm worn out with Baby," replied Mama.

All summer long Noel lay in bed, forgetting how it felt to be well. Sometimes he cried when no one heard him call. Sometimes he slept.

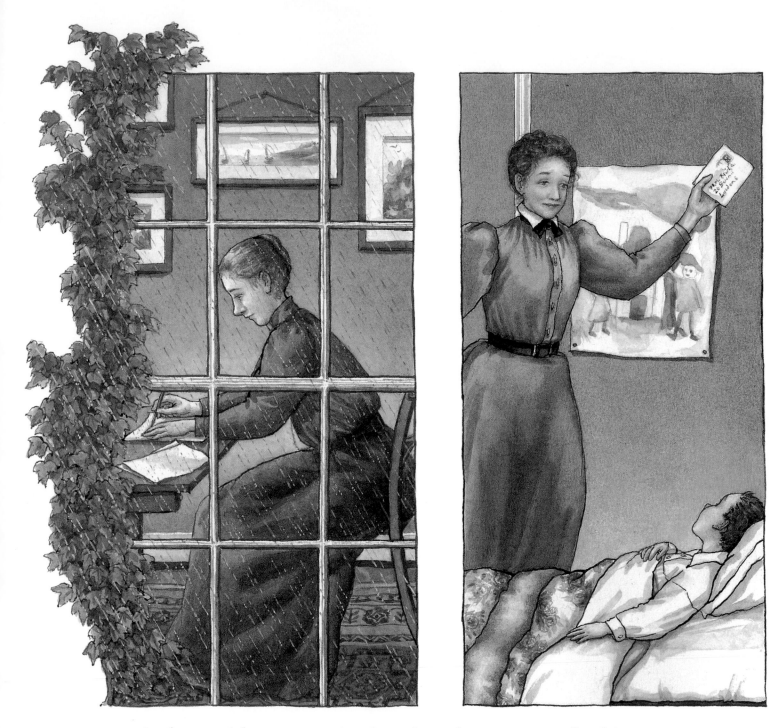

At last, with autumn in the air, a letter came for him.
"See, darling, a fat envelope, full of Miss Potter's news."

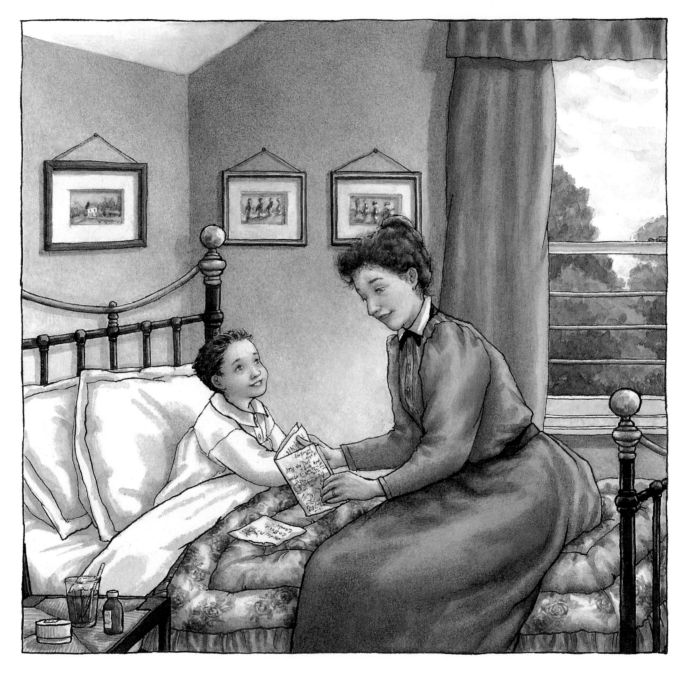

But instead of news, she had sent a *story,* with pictures. And Mama stayed, reading it over and over again, until she was hoarse.

"It's about a rabbit family, but it's just like ours!" exclaimed Noel as the tale began with a mother rabbit and her children. Then, listening to the adventures of the hero, Peter Rabbit, he decided, "It's really about *me*!"

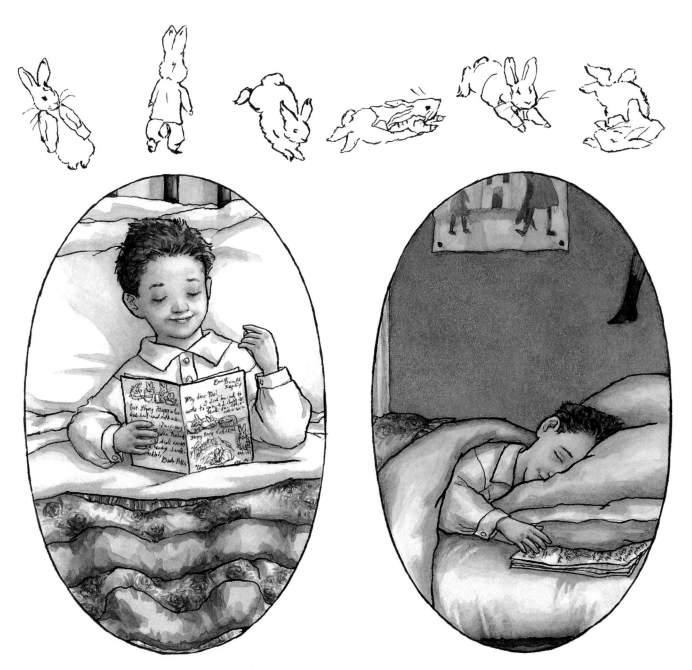

Soon Noel knew the story by heart. He read it to himself whenever he was lonely. It made him laugh. At night he dreamed that he was Peter Rabbit and woke remembering how it felt to run. He wanted to be well.

Within a week he was getting better, and Miss Potter was back.

"You made that story up specially for me?" Noel's eyes grew dark and round as he gazed at his visitor. "Are we best friends?"

Miss Potter smiled. "Of course we are," she said gently. "Best friends."

Noel Moore was a real little boy who lived in London on the edge of Wandsworth Common, a public park. He was five in 1893 when Miss Potter wrote her first story for him. A few years later he was ill again, with polio, and afterwards always walked with a limp.

Quite soon there were eight children in the Moore family and the house was full. Once she had begun, Miss Potter went on writing stories for Noel, Eric and the babies as they grew.

At length, Mrs. Moore had an idea that the tales might be made into books, for other children to enjoy. Pleased with this thought, Miss Potter asked if Noel had kept the very first one. And Noel, who had treasured it for seven years, lent her his letter. With the story made longer and with new, coloured illustrations, *The Tale of Peter Rabbit* was published in 1902.

Although Miss Potter's stories made her famous, she never forgot the Moores, who had been her friends when she was lonely and unknown. Noel grew up to become a priest, helping children in the slums of London and was working among young people at the end of his long life.

Children still read the tales of Beatrix Potter. Perhaps she would never have written them if she had not once known and understood a little boy who needed her. Though far from him, she found the way to reach him and children all over the world.

Eastwood Dunkeld
Sep 4th 93

My dear Noel,
    I don't know what to write to you, so I shall tell you a story about four little rabbits. whose names were —

Flopsy, Mopsy Cottontail

and Peter

They lived with their mother in a sand bank under the root of a big fir tree.

'Now, my dears', said old Mrs Bunny 'you may go into the field or down the lane, but don't go into Mr McGregor's garden.'

Flopsy, Mopsy & Cottontail, who were good little rabbits went down the lane to gather blackberries, but Peter, who was very naughty

---

ran straight away to Mr McGregor's garden and squeezed underneath the gate.
    First he ate some lettuce, and some broad beans, then some radishes, and then, feeling rather sick, he went to look for some parsley; but round the end of a cucumber frame whom should he meet but Mr McGregor!

Mr McGregor was planting out young cabbages but he jumped up & ran after Peter waving a rake & calling out 'stop thief'!

Peter was most dreadfully frightened & rushed all over the garden, for he had forgotten the way back to the gate. He lost one of his shoes among the cabbages